# A MOUSE IN THE CITY

In New York City, U.S.A.

You will never get away, Otis Mouse!

That is what you think.

I can hide in the museum.

This was not a good idea.

Otis jumps on the subway train.

That was a close call!

Atop the Empire State Building:

I live here in New York City.

That is so cool!

Otis sees the cat—again!

Where is that mouse?

Now I'm safe.

Free at last... I hope.

Soon Otis is fast asleep.

The shoe gets packed in a suitcase.

The suitcase is put into a taxi …

Please take me to the airport.

… and then onto a plane.

Last call for flight 339.

When Otis wakes up...

Where in the world am I?

Do I need glasses?

Everything seems ... strange.

Otis is in Egypt.

This is *so* not New York!

# FAR FROM HOME

Otis wants to go back to New York.

I can hide in the shoe until its owner goes home.

Oh, no! He left! I have to find the man with the brown shoes!

I bet he went sightseeing.

Otis follows the man to the Sphinx ...

… and then to the pyramids.

Inside a pyramid:

Uh oh! Now where did he go?

I hear someone crying.

Squeak!

Squeak!

What's the matter?

I am Nuru. My tail is stuck.

Please help me.

The lid is too heavy to lift.

Otis finds something more his size.

Back in the pyramid:

Nuru! Where are you?

I wish I had a map.

The pictures on the wall help Otis.

There is the the tomb!

Otis tries to free Nuru.

Nuru is free!

Otis and Nuru run back to the café.

The man with the brown shoe is gone.

How will I get back to New York?

I can help you get back to New York.

# OTIS ON THE GO

At the bazaar:

Here we are.

A snake! Get me out of here!

Do not worry. The snake charmer has put the snake into a trance.

At lunch:

Look, it is that nice snake.

He is not in a trance anymore!

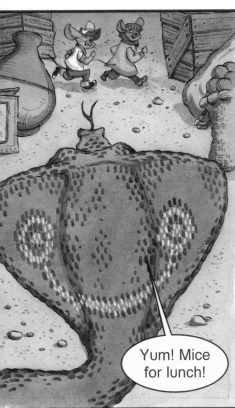

Yum! Mice for lunch!

Hide behind the crates!

Otis is trapped!

This is my lucky day.

I do not want to be a snake's lunch!

SNAKE FLUTES

Nuru has an idea.

This is no time for a concert!

Nuru puts the snake into a trance.

Keep playing, Nuru! It is working.

Otis and Nuru look around.

The Nile is the longest river in the world. It is about 4,130 miles (6,650 km), which is twice the width of the United States.

**Cairo**

*Egypt*

**Luxor**

The Egyptian pyramids were royal tombs. The kings and queens of ancient Egypt were buried in them.

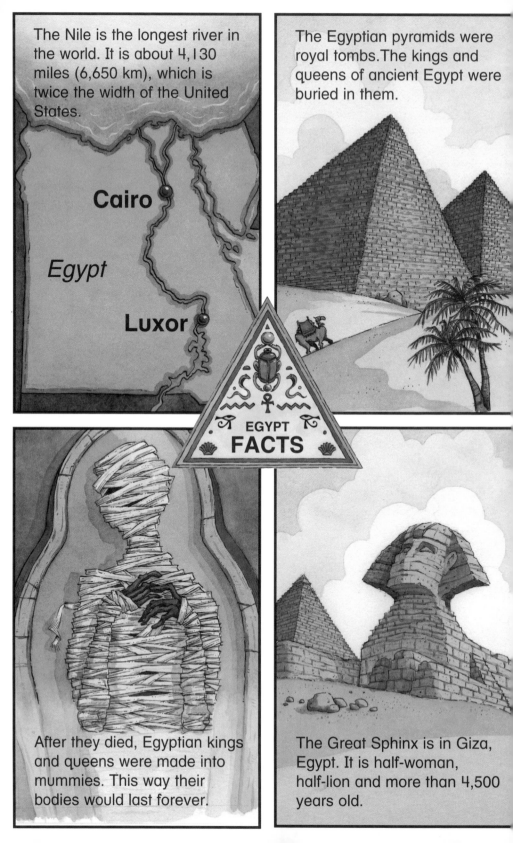

EGYPT
**FACTS**

After they died, Egyptian kings and queens were made into mummies. This way their bodies would last forever.

The Great Sphinx is in Giza, Egypt. It is half-woman, half-lion and more than 4,500 years old.